I0605709

LIVE LIKE A TUDOR

DISCOVERING THE SECRETS OF THE TUDORS

CLAIRE SAUNDERS

ILLUSTRATION

MIA UNDERWOOD

Button Books

CONTENTS

WHO WERE THE TUDORS?

The Tudors were a royal family who ruled England between 1485 and 1603. Three generations of Tudors sat on the throne, including two of the most famous monarchs in English history: King Henry VIII and his daughter Queen Elizabeth I.

The *Mary Rose*, an Elizabethan warship

A time of change

The Tudor Age was a time of great change in England. New ideas about religion began to take hold, sparking huge upheaval. European merchants and explorers sailed across oceans and encountered new lands and other peoples, setting up colonies and trade routes. Cities grew bigger, the first theatres opened, and poetry and literature flourished. By the end of the period, England was becoming an important country. But while some people grew wealthy and enjoyed an easier life, others remained desperately poor.

Playwright and poet William Shakespeare (1564–1616)

A Tudor friend

My name is Mary. I am 11 years old and I live with my family in a beautiful manor house in England. My older sister, Eleanor, is a maid of honour to Queen Elizabeth, and my mother says one day I might join my sister at court. Join me and let me share my life with you. You can take part in my family's Christmas celebrations, watch a play at one of London's new playhouses, and come with me to court to meet the Queen!

A Tudor family tree

This family tree shows the five Tudor kings and queens and the dates they ruled. Lady Jane Grey is sometimes also counted as a Tudor monarch, but she only ruled for nine days and was never crowned.

Henry VII
(1485–1509)

Henry VII seized the throne after decades of war. He brought peace, stability and wealth to the country.

Arthur

Henry VIII (1509-1547)

Henry VII's dashing son (right) became king when he was 18. He loved sports, dancing, music and feasting. He is famous for marrying six times.

Margaret

James V of Scotland

Mary Queen of Scots

James I of England (VI of Scotland)

Mary

Frances

Lady Jane Grey (1553)

The 'nine-day queen' was a great-granddaughter of Henry VII.

Mary I
(1553–1558)

Mary was the child of Henry VIII's first wife, Catherine of Aragon. She earned the nickname 'Bloody Mary' after persecuting people who did not share her Catholic beliefs.

Elizabeth I
(1558–1603)

Elizabeth was the child of Henry VIII's second wife, Anne Boleyn. She never married and was a strong, clever and ruthless ruler.

Edward VI
(1547–1553)

Edward was the child of Henry VIII's third wife, Jane Seymour. He came to the throne when he was just nine years old, so a council of noblemen helped him to rule. Edward died after a short reign.

TIMELINE OF THE TUDORS

The Tudor Age began in 1485, when Henry Tudor won his crown, and ended 118 years later with the death of his granddaughter, Elizabeth I. Here are some of the main events and changes that took place during the reign of the Tudors.

1485
Henry Tudor wins the Battle of Bosworth Field. His victory ends decades of civil war between two of England's most powerful families, the Yorks and the Lancasters, who both claimed the throne. Henry (a Lancaster) becomes King Henry VII, and marries Elizabeth of York to unite the two houses.

1536–1541
Henry VIII seizes the land and wealth of hundreds of Catholic monasteries and convents. This is known as the dissolution of the monasteries.

Henry VII
(ruled 1485–1509)

Henry VIII
(ruled 1509–1547)

Edward VI
(ruled 1547–1553)

1534
For most of Henry VIII's reign, England is a Catholic country, led by the Pope in Rome. But when Henry wants to divorce his first wife and marry someone else, the Pope won't allow it. So Henry breaks away from the Catholic Church and becomes head of the new Church of England, meaning he is free to remarry.

1535–1542
The English parliament passes the Acts of Union with Wales. English becomes the first language of Wales, and Welsh laws are replaced by English ones.

1553
After a short reign, the boy king Edward VI dies, having chosen his cousin, Lady Jane Grey, to be queen after him. She, like him, follows the Protestant religion. But Jane reigns for just nine days before Edward's Catholic half-sister, Mary, takes the throne and Jane is executed.

1565
Sir Thomas Gresham, a wealthy merchant, sets up the Royal Exchange – London's first purpose-built centre for trading stocks. Several floors are later added to house shops, creating England's first shopping mall!

1580
Francis Drake becomes the first Englishman to sail all the way around the world, looting Spanish ships and ports along the way.

1587
A plot is uncovered to kill Elizabeth I and place her cousin, Mary Queen of Scots (the Queen of Scotland), on the throne. Mary is executed for treason.

Around 1591
Shakespeare's first plays are performed in London.

Elizabeth I
(ruled 1558–1603)

Mary I
(ruled 1553–1558)

1558
Elizabeth I is crowned. Her long reign is sometimes called a 'Golden Age'.

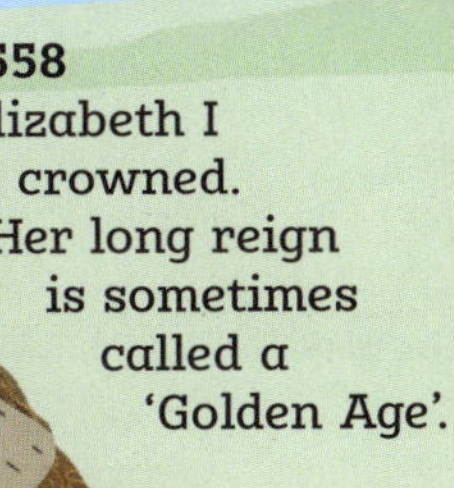

1588
Spain attacks England with a fleet of around 130 ships, called the Spanish Armada. Elizabeth I's gun-armed warships win a famous victory, thanks to better ships, better tactics and a fortunate storm.

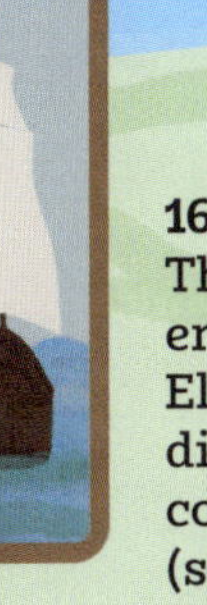

1603
The Tudor Age ends when Elizabeth I dies, and her cousin James I (son of Mary Queen of Scots), becomes king.

TUDOR SOCIETY

In Tudor England, everyone believed in something called the Great Chain of Being – the idea that God had created a natural order for everything in the universe. Most people accepted their position in life, and there was little movement between the different social groups.

A man's world

Tudor England was ruled by female monarchs for half a century, but that did not mean that ordinary women had the same rights as men. Women could not own land or property or go to university. Men were the head of the household, and anything a wife owned or earned belonged to her husband.

The wealthy and middle classes

People believed that the king or queen had been chosen by God.

King or queen

Dukes, earls and other nobles with titles owned big country estates and huge amounts of land. Some noblemen served on the Privy Council, advising the king or queen. The next rank down were the gentry. They were wealthy landowners, but they didn't have titles.

Nobles and gentry

In the middle of Tudor society were yeomen, merchants and craftspeople. Yeomen were fairly well-off farmers who owned their own land and could afford to employ labourers on the farm.

Middle society

The poor

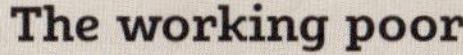

The working poor

The poorest members of society included servants, tenant farmers (who rented land from wealthy landowners) and labourers. Working days were long and life could be tough.

At the bottom of society were poor people who could not afford to feed themselves and were forced to beg.

Vagrants and the unemployed

Help for the poor

The number of poor people exploded in the Tudor Age. To tackle the problem, Queen Elizabeth I put in place a series of Poor Laws from 1563 to 1601. The old, young, sick and disabled were looked after, and people who were fit and healthy but unable to find jobs were put to work. Those who refused to work – the so-called 'idle' (lazy) poor – were punished harshly.

Black Tudors

Historians know of over 200 people of African heritage living in Tudor England. Some arrived as traders from Africa, others came via Spain or Portugal. They worked mainly as servants but some did other jobs. One man, John Blanke, was a trumpeter in Henry VIII's court. These people all lived freely in England. But elsewhere, English traders were beginning their involvement in the terrible transatlantic slave trade (see page 27).

EVERYDAY JOBS

Tudor jobs generally involved a lot of hard work and very little money. There was no retirement either – people worked until they were too old or ill to carry on. Most people made their living from farming, but there were lots of other jobs too. Here are just a few of them.

Spinster

Spinning wool was a woman's job. In the countryside, many women (and their children) earned a bit of money this way. Using a spinning wheel or a spindle, they transformed clumps of wool into fine strands of yarn. This was later woven into cloth on looms.

Merchant

Merchants sailed to Europe to buy and sell goods, and some became very wealthy. English cloth made up 90 percent of their exports – it was reckoned to be the finest in Europe.

Women were often involved in the family business but, generally, only widows were allowed to run their own businesses.

Make butter like a Tudor

Some girls and women worked as dairy maids, milking cows and making butter and cheese. They made butter by skimming the cream off the milk, and then stirring this in a butter churner. You can make butter the same way. Pour 3½fl oz (100ml) of double cream into a clean jam jar, screw the lid on tightly and shake. After 8–10 minutes, the cream will separate into liquid (buttermilk) and a ball of butter. Drain off the liquid, tip out the butter and squeeze out any extra liquid, then rinse under cold water. Add salt to taste.

Barber

Barbers didn't just cut hair and shave people – they also pulled out rotten teeth, bled patients (see p.35) and carried out minor operations.

Scullion

Scullions were kitchen workers who did all the dirtiest jobs – scouring pots and pans, scrubbing filthy floors and stoves, plucking the feathers from birds, and turning the cooking spits by the hot fireplace.

Craftsperson

Tudor towns and cities were full of skilled craftspeople – carpenters, shoe makers, bookbinders, pin makers, wheelwrights (wheel makers), and many more. They worked from their homes or workshops, and sometimes sold what they made from shops at the front of their houses. Different trades were organized into groups called guilds.

Gong farmer

Gong farmers had one of the worst jobs in Tudor England. Using a bucket and spade, they shovelled and scraped out human waste from privies (toilets) and cesspits, before carting it out of the city. The job was so stinky that the men were only allowed to work at night!

RELIGION AND BELIEFS

Religion was a very important part of people's lives in Tudor times. Everybody believed in God, went to church every week (it became the law under Edward VI) and prayed every day. So when huge religious changes shook the country, everyone's everyday lives were affected.

Catholics and Protestants

In the 16th century, change swept through Christian Churches in Europe. Some people began to criticize the wealthy, all-powerful Catholic Church, and set up new Protestant Churches instead. This religious movement was called the Reformation. There were many differences between the Catholic and Protestant Churches. Here are some of them:

Catholic

Church services and the Bible were in Latin, which few people understood.

Protestant

Church services and the Bible were in English, which ordinary people could understand. This meant they could read and interpret the Bible for themselves for the first time.

Catholic

The Pope was head of the Church.

Protestant

In England, the king or queen was head of the Church.

Catholic

Churches were highly decorated.

Protestant

Churches were plain. In Edward's reign, when churches in England changed from Catholic to Protestant, altars and statues were smashed and wall paintings were painted over.

All change!

During the Reformation in England, the country swung violently from one religion to another and back again, depending on whether the king or queen of the time was Catholic or Protestant. Everyone in the country had to follow the same religion as their monarch or risk being punished, imprisoned or even killed. Imagine being told what to believe, under pain of death! Some people were prepared to die for their beliefs rather than give them up.

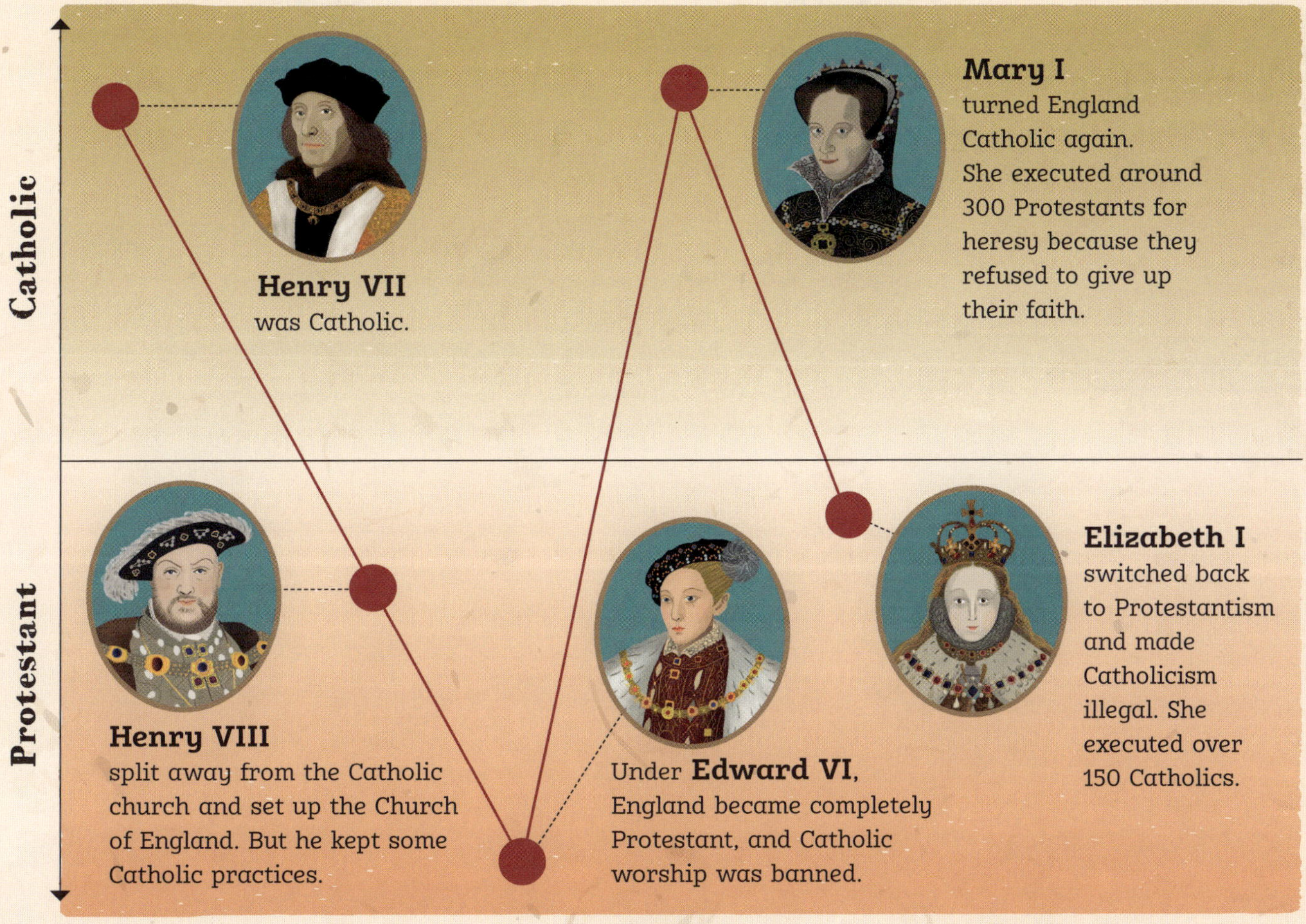

Catholic

Protestant

Henry VII was Catholic.

Henry VIII split away from the Catholic church and set up the Church of England. But he kept some Catholic practices.

Under **Edward VI**, England became completely Protestant, and Catholic worship was banned.

Mary I turned England Catholic again. She executed around 300 Protestants for heresy because they refused to give up their faith.

Elizabeth I switched back to Protestantism and made Catholicism illegal. She executed over 150 Catholics.

Superstition

People in Tudor times were very superstitious. It was perfectly normal to believe in witches, ghosts, fairies and mischievous goblins, and to wear a lucky charm to ward off danger. Many things were thought to bring good or bad luck, such as walking under a ladder (bad), touching wood (good) or even being breathed on by a cow (good, supposedly!) Saying 'bless you' when a person sneezed was thought to stop the Devil sneaking into their open mouth.

CHILDHOOD AND FAMILY LIFE

In a Tudor family everyone knew their place. The father was the head of the household, and the mother's job was to be a good housewife. Parents were generally much stricter than they are today, and children were expected to be respectful and obedient – or else!

The early years

Having a baby in Tudor times was a dangerous business. It wasn't unusual for women to die in childbirth, and one in seven babies sadly did not make it to their first birthday.

Newborns were wrapped tightly from head to toe in long bands of material called swaddling, so they couldn't move – people thought this would make the baby's arms and legs grow straight and healthy. When they were finally released, wheeled baby-walkers allowed them to whizz around enjoying their new-found freedom!

Up until the age of five or so, girls and boys were dressed the same, in long-skirted gowns. After that, they wore miniature versions of adult clothing.

Tudor toys and games

Tudor children played with lots of different toys. There were wooden dolls, metal figures of knights on horseback, spinning tops, hobby-horses for riding and hoops that could be raced along the ground using sticks. Backgammon and chess were played in wealthy families, while children of all classes enjoyed the board game Nine Men's Morris – you can learn how to play it yourself on page 40.

Bow and curtsey like a Tudor!

From a young age, children were expected to show respect to adults by curtseying (girls) or bowing (boys). Have a go yourself and see if you can master the moves!

Girls: Lower your eyes and bend your knees outwards, keeping your back straight, with your arms slightly out to the side.

Boys: Take off your hat using your right hand (use an imaginary hat if you don't have one), then switch it to your left hand and hold it by your body. Sweep your right arm out as you bring one foot back and bend your knees, tilting your body forward slightly.

Good manners

In well-off families, learning good manners and the rules of behaviour were an important part of growing up. Instruction manuals aimed at upper-class boys and girls laid out some of the rules. Children had to learn how to eat, dress and talk in a certain way – and even how to sit, stand and walk using the correct posture and movements.

All of these manners showed a person's position in society, and it was important to get them right.

A tight squeeze!

Tudor households were generally bigger than they are today. Families sometimes took in relatives, such as unmarried aunts, orphaned cousins or elderly grandparents. There were often also servants and apprentices living with the family, sharing bedrooms, meals and day-to-day life. No one would have had much privacy!

EDUCATION

Not many children went to school in Tudor England. There was no free education – it was mostly only boys from well-off families who could afford the fees. Girls and the sons of nobles were taught at home, while the poorest children had to work instead, helping their parents in the house or on the farm.

Children learnt to write using goose-quill pens dipped into pots of ink. The quills were sharpened with special knives called 'penknives'.

Home education

At home, girls learnt all the skills needed to be a housewife. This could include reading and writing, but also sewing and cooking. Noble girls would learn singing, dancing and playing musical instruments. Girls generally did not learn Latin and Greek, and were barred from university.

Boys started at 'petty schools' when they were around four, learning to read and write, then moved to grammar school aged seven. There, boys of different ages studied Latin and Greek, religious books and mathematics. They mostly learnt by rote, which means repeating information to memorize it.

The number of schools increased in the Tudor Age. At the start of the period, just five percent of men and one percent of women could read and write. By the end of the 1500s, this had risen to 25 percent of men and 10 percent of women.

School days were long, from around 6am (or 7am in winter) until 5pm, and there was only one day off a week. Schoolmasters were allowed to use birch twigs to beat boys who misbehaved.

Leaving home

Children from both rich and poor families often finished their childhood away from home and spent their teenage years living with another family.

Girls and boys from wealthy homes were sometimes sent away to live with a higher-status relative, in the hope they would meet influential people or make a good marriage.

Middle-income families might pay for their teenage sons to become an apprentice and learn a trade. Apprenticeships usually lasted for seven years. Boys lived with their master while they trained, and were treated as part of the family. Apprenticeships for girls did exist, but were very rare.

Children whose families couldn't afford apprenticeships often spent their teenage years working as live-in servants. They lived with a family in the local area, helping in the fields or with household jobs for a small wage.

Some villages had small, informal schools ran by local women. These offered very basic lessons to poorer children, both boys and girls.

24 HOURS AS A TUDOR

Daily life in Tudor England was very different for wealthy people and poor people. But this is what might have happened to our girl from a wealthy family on a typical day.

6.30am: washing and dressing

Mary rinses her face and hands in cold water, combs her hair and cleans her teeth using a tooth cloth and tooth powder made from cloves. A servant helps to lace her into her clothes.

6am: wake up

Mary wakes up in a bed she shares with her sister. Her cousin sleeps in the same room. All the girls start the day by saying morning prayers.

8am: church

After breakfast, Mary's family take a horse-drawn carriage to church. By law, everyone in the country has to go to church once a week, but many people go more often.

10am: music practice

It's time for Mary's music lesson. Girls from upper-class families are expected to be able to dance gracefully, sing and play musical instruments. Today Mary is practising the lute.

11.30am: dinner

Dinner is the main meal of the day. There are two courses, each with several dishes. Today there is no meat, only fish, because it's a Friday, which is a fasting day. Mary makes sure she is sitting up straight and doesn't speak with her mouth full – her mother will be keeping an eye on her table manners!

1pm: walk in the garden

After dinner, the girls walk in the garden and watch Mary's brothers practise archery.

2pm: sewing

Mary works on her sampler – a piece of embroidery that shows off all the different sewing skills and stitches she has learned.

5pm: supper and games

Supper is another formal two-course meal. Afterwards, Mary plays chess with her brother.

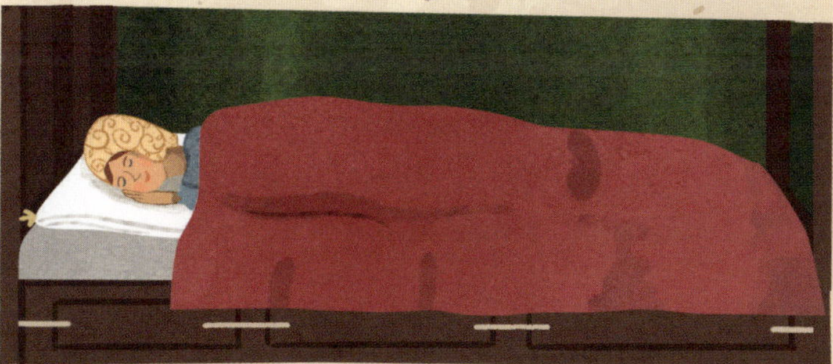

7pm: bed

After saying her prayers, Mary climbs into bed. She lies down on her right side as this is considered healthiest for sleeping. Her bed feels a bit saggy – tomorrow the servants will need to take off the mattress and tighten the ropes strung across the bed's wooden frame.

Midnight: end of 'first sleep'

Mary wakes up from her 'first sleep'. For an hour or so, she chats to her sister before going back to sleep. Many people in Tudor times split their sleep into two halves, broken up by an hour or two of being awake. In this time, they might read, pray, chat, or even do work or household chores!

EMBROIDER A TUDOR ROSE

All Tudor girls were taught how to sew. Those from poorer families learnt simple, practical sewing skills, such as mending and making clothes, while girls from wealthier families spent hours practising embroidery (intricate decorations stitched onto fabric). Some men worked as embroiderers too. Have a go at embroidering a Tudor rose and put your needlework skills to the test.

The Tudor Rose

The Tudor Age began when Henry VII won the civil war being fought between the York and Lancaster families (see page 6). This war later became known as the War of the Roses, because the House of York was represented by a red rose and the House of Lancaster by a white rose. When Henry VII (a Lancaster) married Elizabeth of York, the symbols of the two houses were merged to create a brand-new symbol: the Tudor Rose. In the sixteenth century, this symbol appeared on buildings, in paintings and on coins. Today it is an emblem of England.

You will need

- **a piece of hessian, around 12in by 12in (30cm by 30cm)**
- **marker pen**
- **small balls of yellow, white, red and green yarn**
- **darning needle (a blunt needle with a large hole)**
- **thread, around 20in (50cm)**
- **scissors**
- **string, around 20in (50cm)**

1 Draw the outline of a Tudor Rose onto the hessian.

Start by drawing a circle around 1⅛in (3cm) across, then draw five short petals around it.

Add five outer petals.

Finally, add five small pointy leaves.

2 Start by embroidering the centre circle. Thread the needle with the yellow yarn and tie a knot in the end. Push the needle through the back of the hessian to the front, then begin to make short stitches around the outside of the circle, slowly working your way into the centre.

3 Next, embroider the five inner petals. Using the white yarn, make long stitches from the inside of each petal to the outside.

4 Now embroider the five outer petals. Using the red yarn, make long stitches from the inside of each petal to the outside.

5 To finish the rose, embroider the five small leaves. Using the green yarn, make stitches from the middle of the leaf to the outside edge, then repeat for the other half of the leaf.

6 Using the red yarn, stitch a border around your Tudor rose. Then trim off any extra hessian fabric, leaving 2–4in (5–10cm) of spare fabric at the top.

7 Flip over the hessian. Place the length of string near the top edge and fold the hessian down over it. Then use the needle and the thread to stitch down the hessian.

8 Once you have tied the string, your Tudor rose embroidery is ready to be hung up and admired!

Place your finished embroidery under a pile of books overnight to flatten the hessian before you hang it up.

A TUDOR VILLAGE

Most people in Tudor England lived in villages in the countryside and made their living from farming. Often, they lived very simple lives, never travelling much further than the nearest market town. Here is what a typical Tudor village might have looked like.

Tudor towns

In the Tudor Age, towns grew larger as more and more people began to live in them. The biggest city in England was London, the centre of government and trade. Between 1500 and 1600, its population soared from 50,000 to 200,000. Most towns though were very small compared to today – just a few thousand people.

London and other big towns were bustling, noisy and smelly. Filthy, narrow streets were crowded with people and crammed with tall, slender buildings that blocked out the light. Often, tradespeople or craftsmen of the same trade (such as butchers, wool sellers or goldsmiths) lived and work in the same street or part of town.

At the local mill, grain was ground into flour for making bread. Not all houses had ovens, so many villages had bakehouses where people could take their bread dough to be baked.
Nobles and the gentry lived on big country estates.
Passing travellers spent the night at the inn.
Inn
The stocks were used as a punishment for small crimes or bad behaviour.
Well
Streets were muddy dirt tracks. People travelled between villages or towns on foot or on horseback. Only wealthy Tudors used carriages.
Larger villages might hold a regular market.
Farmers grew wheat, oats, barley, peas and beans in the fields around the village. They used horses or oxen to pull the heavy ploughs, and kept sheep for their wool, milk and meat. Cows were milked twice a day and the milk was made into butter and cheese.

INSIDE A TUDOR TOWNHOUSE

The houses of ordinary people began to become a bit more comfortable during the Tudor Age. Those who could afford it added chimneys, glass windows and upper floors for the first time. More rooms meant more private space. This is what a typical merchant's town house might have looked like.

Many poor people still lived in simple huts with one or two rooms and an open hearth in the middle of the room. Smoke escaped through the thatched roof and windows.

Bed mattresses were laid on ropes strung across a wooden frame. The ropes could be tightened if they started to sag.

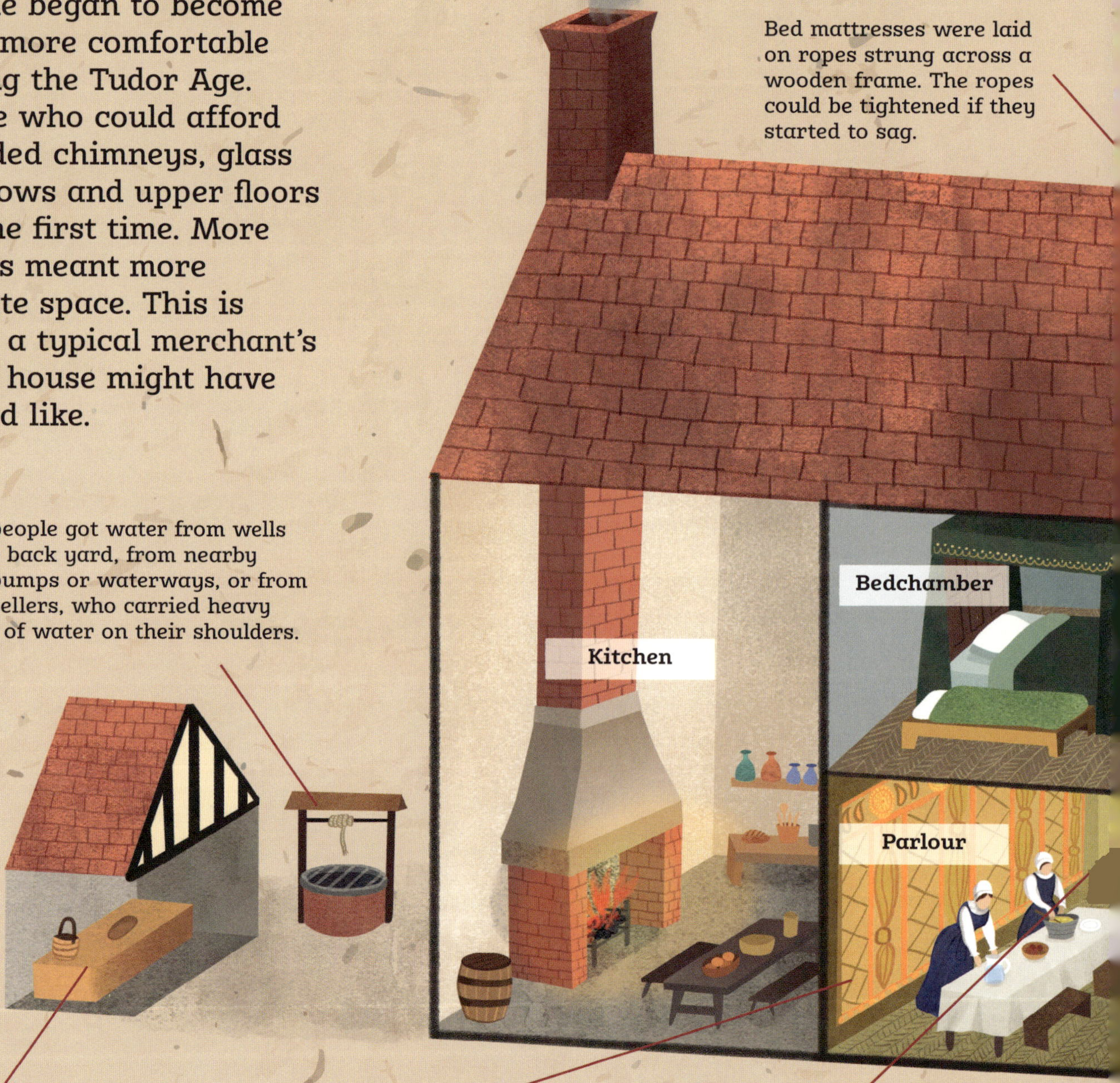

Townspeople got water from wells in their back yard, from nearby street pumps or waterways, or from water sellers, who carried heavy barrels of water on their shoulders.

Kitchen

Bedchamber

Parlour

Some houses had privies (toilets) in the back yard. These were just holes in the ground, which were covered with a wooden bench.

Tapestries or colourful painted cloths hung from the walls.

People lit their houses with candles made of tallow (animal fat) or beeswax (which was more expensive). Poor people used rushlights (rushes dipped in animal fat) instead.

Tudor houses had a wooden frame filled in with wattle-and-daub (woven sticks and plaster) or brick. In towns, houses generally had tiled roofs, rather than thatch, because of the risk of fire.

Four-poster beds had curtains to keep out draughts and for privacy. Sharing a bedroom was common, especially for children and servants.

Some houses had overhanging upper storeys called jetties. These gave people more living space.

At night, people used chamber pots, which were often emptied out straight onto the street!

Glass windows became more common in the Tudor Age, although they were expensive – if someone moved house they took the glass with them! Those who couldn't afford glass covered their windows with shutters made of wood or oiled cloth.

Furniture was big, heavy and home-made. Pieces of furniture, like beds and chairs, were expensive and expected to last – they were handed down through generations.

The floor was covered with a thick layer of rushes. These could be changed when they got dirty.

In towns, many houses had shops on the ground floor. These opened on to the street, so that craftspeople and tradespeople could sell their goods to passers-by.

The 'New World'
European explorers wanted to find a route to Asia across the Atlantic Ocean – they thought if they sailed across it they would eventually arrive in China. Instead, they discovered two continents they had not known existed: South America and North America. One of the first European explorers to reach the Americas was John Cabot, on an expedition organized by Henry VII in 1497. He landed in what is now Canada.

Colonies
Spain and Portugal were the first countries to set up colonies in the Americas, seizing the land and wealth of the Indigenous people who lived there. Elizabeth I attempted to set up her own colonies on the east coast of North America, starting with Roanoke Island in 1585. However, none succeeded, and it was only after her death that a permanent settlement was founded, in Jamestown, Virginia, in 1607.

North America

Atlantic Ocean

South America

EXPLORATION AND TRADE

The 15th and 16th centuries were a great age of European exploration. With Portugal and Spain leading the way, the kings and queens of Europe sent ships on long sea voyages into the unknown, to search for new trade routes and distant lands. These expeditions brought great wealth to Tudor England.

Map key

- Drake circumnavigation, 1577–1580
- Cabot's route, 1497
- Roanoke Island colony, 1585 (abandoned)

An English navy
England didn't just need ships for trade and exploration, but also to defend itself from attack. Henry VIII built dockyards and dozens of fast warships fitted with the latest guns. This was England's first permanent navy.

Trade
The discovery of new sea routes opened up trading opportunities for merchants in Elizabethan England. Now, ships were able to sail far beyond the shores of Europe, to North Africa, the Americas and around the southern tip of Africa to the Far East. English merchants traded woollen cloth for luxury goods such as silk, spices and sugar.

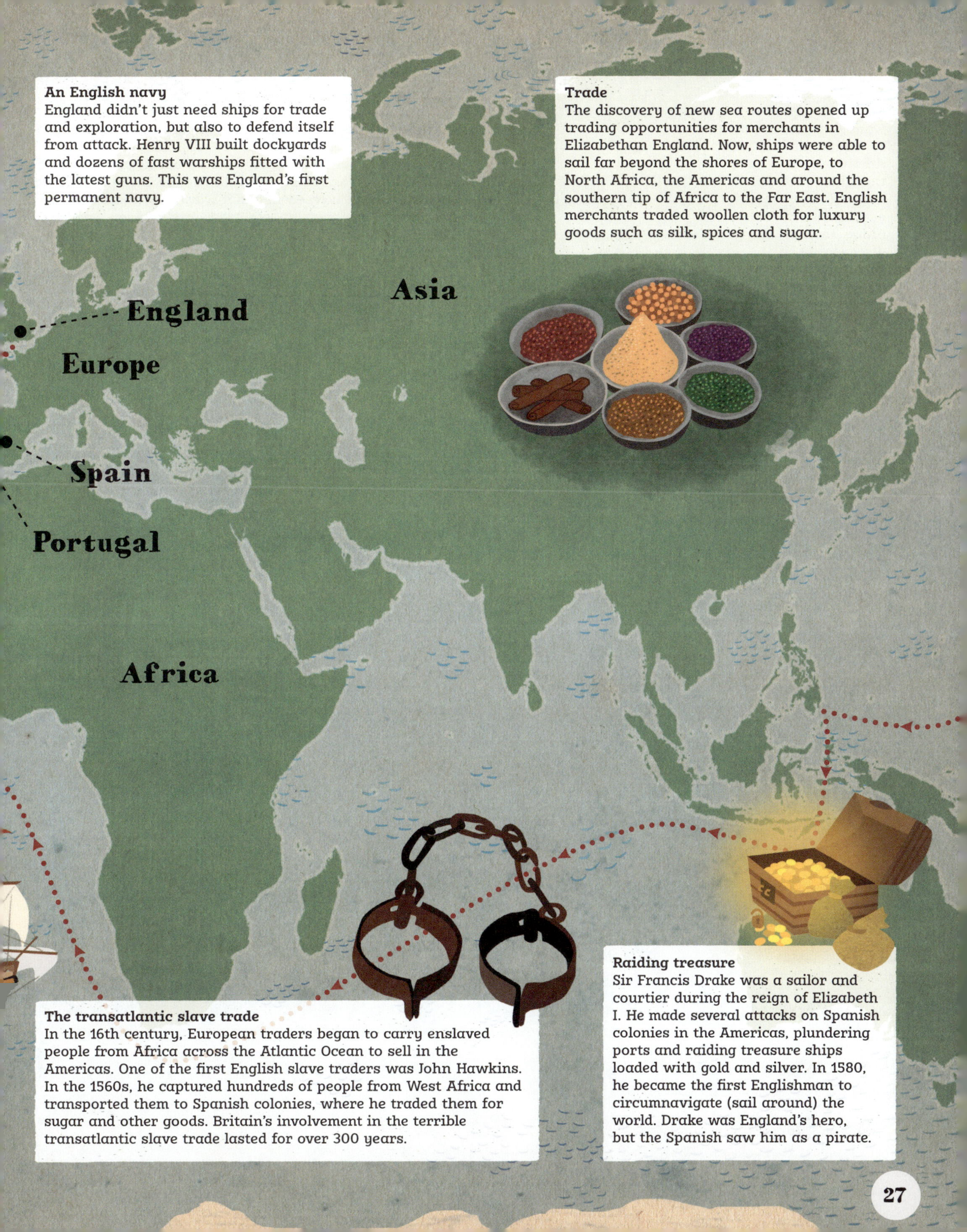

Asia

England

Europe

Spain

Portugal

Africa

The transatlantic slave trade
In the 16th century, European traders began to carry enslaved people from Africa across the Atlantic Ocean to sell in the Americas. One of the first English slave traders was John Hawkins. In the 1560s, he captured hundreds of people from West Africa and transported them to Spanish colonies, where he traded them for sugar and other goods. Britain's involvement in the terrible transatlantic slave trade lasted for over 300 years.

Raiding treasure
Sir Francis Drake was a sailor and courtier during the reign of Elizabeth I. He made several attacks on Spanish colonies in the Americas, plundering ports and raiding treasure ships loaded with gold and silver. In 1580, he became the first Englishman to circumnavigate (sail around) the world. Drake was England's hero, but the Spanish saw him as a pirate.

A VISIT TO COURT

The murky waters of the River Thames slap noisily against the sides of the boat as we approach the landing stage. I gaze up at the high walls of Whitehall Palace and take a deep breath. Today I am meeting Queen Elizabeth, and I am so nervous it feels like eels are wriggling in my stomach. My mother hopes I will make a good impression and the Queen will allow me to join my sister, Eleanor, at court when I am a little older. Eleanor is a maid of honour in the Queen's chamber. I hope the Queen is in a good mood – my mother has warned me that her tongue can be sharp and her temper hot.

My legs wobble as my mother and I climb off the boat onto shore. I just have time to smooth out my skirts before we are swept up the steps and into the palace. My father once told me that Whitehall has over 1,500 rooms and is the largest palace in all of Europe! Many times he has described to me the beautiful gardens, the great hall lit up with a thousand candles, the tiltyard where brave lords joust, and the tennis court where my grandfather once played tennis with the Queen's father, Henry VIII.

We walk through room after beautiful room, past strolling courtiers, hurrying servants and stern-faced guards, until we arrive at the Presence Chamber. When the door opens and we walk in, my heart trembles. There is the Queen, dressed in a magnificent gown studded with pearls, her hair glowing fiery red in the sunlight that slants into the room. But her brows are drawn together into a frown, and her voice, when she welcomes us, sounds sharp. The Queen is not in a good mood!

I sink into a curtsey before her, and my mother offers our gift, a pair of sapphire earrings. The Queen inclines her head graciously but does not smile. Instead, she sinks back into her chair, sighs irritably, and then turns her eyes on me. 'Perhaps YOU can entertain me,' she says, and she signals one of her ladies to pass me a lute. Holding the instrument in my clammy hands, I settle myself on a stool, but my mind is horribly blank – what shall I play? But then I have an idea. I pluck the strings, and the room fills with the notes of a song written by the Queen's father, Henry VIII, 'Pastime with good company'. For the first time, a smile creeps onto the Queen's face and her face softens. I silently give thanks for all those long hours of music practice. I have pleased the Queen! My family will be so proud.

TUDOR FASHION

Clothes were very important to the Tudors. The style, colour and material of a person's clothes made it instantly clear to others how important they were in society. There were even laws, called sumptuary laws, that set out what people of certain classes were and weren't allowed to wear.

Costly clothing

Most people didn't own many clothes. Everything had to be sewn by hand, which took a lot of time and meant clothes were expensive. People who could afford it might save up and visit a tailor, while others made their own clothes or bought them second-hand. Clothes were looked after carefully, mended until they fell apart and even passed on in people's wills!

Many pieces of clothing, such as collars, cuffs and sleeves, came in separate parts, so that they could be attached to different outfits using laces threaded through matching holes or lots of pins. Getting dressed could take some time!

Tudor pin

Outfit for a working woman

Underwear was a long linen smock, which was washed regularly

In cold weather or on special occasions, a long-sleeved gown would be worn over the top of this outfit.

A pestle and mortar for grinding ingredients

Tudor make-up

Pale skin was a sign of nobility in Tudor times. Some wealthy women, including Queen Elizabeth I, used a mixture of white lead and vinegar to make their skin smooth and white. Unfortunately, the mixture was very toxic and caused skin problems – which were then covered up by more toxic make-up!

Outfits for a noble couple (1540s)

Hat

Linen undershirt with ruffles and embroidery

Robe

Doublet (jacket)

Round hose (trousers)

Stockings

Hair covered by hood

Wide sleeves, with separate detachable undersleeves

Jewelled girdle around the waist

Gown of silk or velvet, worn over a kirtle underdress

Boned frame called a farthingale gives the skirt its cone shape

Changing fashions

Fashions changed throughout the Tudor period. In Elizabeth I's reign, elaborately frilled collars called ruffs became popular for the well-off. Women's skirts changed too. They became much wider, with a drum-like shape.

Ruff

Drum-shaped skirt

MAKE A RUFF

In Elizabethan England, everyone who could afford it wore a ruff. Ruffs started out as small ruffles on collars and cuffs, but as time went on, these frills became bigger and more elaborate. Some ruffs were made from metres of fabric and were wider than a person's shoulders! You can make a ruff of your own, with matching cuffs.

A sign of status

Ruffs were made of linen or lace, which was pleated or folded and then stiffened using starch. Sometimes wires and other supports were used too. Ruffs were a sign of status, because it took hours of work to get them ready. Most ruffs were only worn once, and then had to be washed and re-made.

Can you imagine going about your daily life wearing an enormous ruff around your neck, trying not to crush any of the delicate folds? Moving about freely would be very difficult – you certainly wouldn't be able to plough a field or milk a cow! In Tudor times, wearing a ruff showed the world that you were wealthy enough not to have to do any hard physical work and that you had servants to look after your ruffs.

You will need

- **6 sheets of A4 (letter-sized) white paper**
- **Scissors**
- **Hole punch**
- **Glue**
- **3ft (1m) string or ribbon**

1 To make the ruff, fold four pieces of paper in half lengthways, then cut along the folds. You will end up with eight long strips of paper.

2 Fold each of the strips of paper backwards and forwards, making pleats of around ½in (1.2cm).

3 Use a hole punch to make a hole in the middle of the pleats at one end of the paper.

4 Make small snips into the other end of the paper. This will create a lace-like pattern once you unfold the paper. You can copy the pattern opposite, or come up with your own design. Make sure you use the same design on all eight strips of paper.

5 Glue together the ends of each of the eight strips, making sure you line up the holes. You will end up with one long strip of pleated paper.

6 Thread 20in (50cm) of string or ribbon through the holes, then separate out the pleats. Your ruff is complete!

7 To make the cuffs, follow the steps above but use narrower strips of paper. You will need eight narrow strips – four for each cuff. To make them, fold two pieces of the paper in half lengthways, and then in half again, before cutting along the folds.

You can now wear your ruff and cuffs! Ask someone to fasten them around your neck and wrists using a bow.

1
2
3
4
5
6
7

HEALTH AND MEDICINE

Disease was common in Tudor England. Doctors did not understand about germs and good hygiene, so they were not very good at treating illness. Children were especially at risk – in the late Tudor period, around a third of all deaths were children under 10.

Deadly diseases

There were all sorts of infectious diseases to worry about, from dysentery to bubonic plague. Many people died in outbreaks of 'sweating sickness', a mysterious disease that swept the country several times in the Tudor period and killed its victims within hours. Another deadly disease was smallpox, which killed around a third of those it infected, and left some survivors horribly scarred. One of the main ways of diagnosing sickness was by examining and even tasting urine!

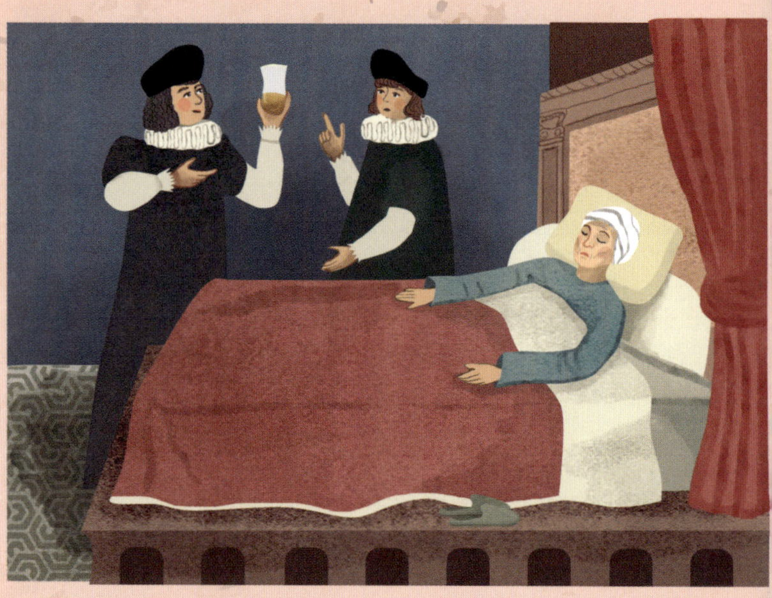

Bad air

The Tudors didn't know about germs and viruses. They thought infections were caused by bad 'vapours' drifting through the air and soaking into the skin. People surrounded themselves with good smells to overpower the dangerous bad ones. They sprinkled scented water on their clothing, hung bundles of herbs in their homes and carried pomanders (small containers that held balls of scent or herbs).

To prevent infection seeping into the pores of their skin, people kept their bodies covered up, used linen 'rubbing cloths' to scrub clean their skin, and changed their underclothes as often as possible!

Humours and herbs

Tudor medicine was based around the idea that there were four 'humours' or fluids in the body that needed to be kept in balance: blood, yellow bile, black bile and phlegm. It was thought that too much of one humour could make you ill.

Doctors prescribed herbal remedies and other treatments to 'rebalance' the humours – for example, someone with too much blood might be 'bled' by having blood-sucking leeches placed on their skin.

Doctors were expensive – a visit might cost several months' salary. So often people went to see an apothecary or a wise woman instead, who would send them away with herbs or potions. There were also barber surgeons who did small operations.

Sugar was so popular among rich people that many ended up with rotten or missing teeth.

Curious cures

Some Tudor medicine was nothing more than superstition. Check out these weird 'cures':

Headache: Press a length of rope to the head.

Jaundice: Drink nine lice mixed with ale every morning for a week.

Smallpox: Hang red curtains around the bed.

Many people believed illnesses were punishments from God or were caused by curses or the positions of the stars.

CRIME AND PUNISHMENT

Anyone caught breaking the law in Tudor times was treated very harshly. Crimes were rarely punished with prison sentences like they are today. Instead people were publicly shamed, whipped, beaten or even killed. People thought this would deter others from committing crime.

Local justice

Tudor England did not have a police force, so it was left up to ordinary people to keep law and order in their community. Some villages and small towns had parish constables. This job was unpaid, and done by farmers and tradesmen on top of their usual work. Parish constables were organized by the local Justice of the Peace (JP), who was generally a rich landowner.

Even minor wrongdoings could be punished harshly. One of the most common crimes was vagrancy – wandering from place to place without a home or job. Vagrants were whipped, burned through the ear and, if they were caught begging again, hanged.

Pillories and stocks were used to humiliate the person being punished. Passers-by jeered and threw things such as rotten fruit at them.

Whipping was a common punishment for small crimes, such as stealing, begging or refusing to attend church, and many towns and villages had a whipping post.

Pillory

Whipping post

Stocks

Cucking stools were used to punish women for 'scolding', gossiping or speaking out of turn. Women were tied to a chair, paraded through the streets and then dunked repeatedly underwater.

Prison time

Some criminals were thrown into prison and held there until their trial took place, and their punishment would be decided. In London, one of the worst prisons was Newgate. It was cold, dirty, crowded, smelly and full of disease. Prisoners had to pay for their room, bedding and food – if they couldn't afford it and no one helped them, they starved.

Wealthy, important prisoners were held in the Tower of London, often in comfortable rooms with servants. Two of Henry VIII's wives and Lady Jane Grey (see p.5) were all imprisoned there before they were executed.

Some prisoners at the Tower of London were tortured. One of the most feared instruments was the rack, which stretched the victim's body, sometimes breaking their bones. Another grim torture device was the Scavenger's Daughter, which was a cage that forced the body into a painfully uncomfortable position.

Off with their head!

Serious crimes, such as murder, heresy (following the wrong religion), treason and stealing items of value, were punished with death. Public executions were popular events that drew huge crowds, even families.

Most people were hanged, although nobles were granted a quicker death, by beheading. Other gruesome execution methods included being boiled alive, burnt at the stake, 'pressed' (crushed to death by heavy stones), or drawn, hanged and quartered (dragged through the streets, and then cut into pieces).

SPORTS AND ENTERTAINMENT

Wealthy Tudors had lots of free time to enjoy sports, grand banquets and other fancy entertainments. Poorer people had to make do with just a few hours off a week, on Sunday afternoons after church. Here are some of the things that the Tudors liked to do for fun.

Jousting

At jousting contests, rich nobles tried to knock each other off their horse. At one tournament, Henry VIII was badly injured when his horse fell on top of him.

Archery was popular with men of all classes. Henry VIII made it the law that every man keep a bow at home and practise on Sundays.

Tennis

In Tudor times, tennis was played on an indoor court in wealthy homes. The ball could be bounced off the walls (a bit like the modern game of squash).

Hunting and hawking

Well-off men and women enjoyed hunting deer and other animals using bows and arrows. Hawking (using birds of prey to catch other birds) was also popular.

Bowling

Bowls was played on village greens and in public bowling alleys, in taverns, palaces and country estates. At one point, Henry VIII passed a law banning ordinary people from bowling – he thought they should be hard at work instead.

Football

The football of Tudor times wasn't like the game we know today. It was usually played between villages across miles of countryside, and involved each team trying to capture the ball and bring it back to their village. The game could involve hundreds of players, and often got quite rough – some people ended up with broken bones! In Wales, football was known as *cnapan*.

Music and dancing

Music and dancing were enjoyed in all parts of Tudor society. Among the nobility, being able to dance elegantly and play a musical instrument were seen as signs of good breeding. Henry VIII even composed his own music. In the countryside, travelling musicians played at markets and village fairs, and lively country dances took place outdoors in the summer.

Holidays

There were many holy days (or 'holidays') throughout the year, when people took a break from work and enjoyed feasts, music, dancing, games, processions and country fairs. Two of the biggest holidays were Christmas (see page 50) and Easter.

Masques were feasts for the rich that included dancing, singing and plays.

Animal blood sports

People from all classes watched cruel, bloodthirsty 'sports' using animals. Cockerels, dogs, bulls and chained-up bears were forced to fight each other in front of cheering crowds. It's hard to imagine now, but this was one of the most popular entertainments in Tudor England.

PLAY TUDOR GAMES

Many of the games that the Tudors enjoyed we still play today, including chess, backgammon and card games. One of the most popular games was called Nine Men's Morris. You can make your own board and challenge a friend to a game.

Make and play Nine Men's Morris

You will need

- Thick cardboard
- Scissors
- A thick black pen

1 Cut out a large square of cardboard, around 12 by 12in (30 by 30cm).

2 Draw on the grid, following the 3 steps opposite.

3 Draw and cut out 18 small circles, and colour half of them black. These are the counters.

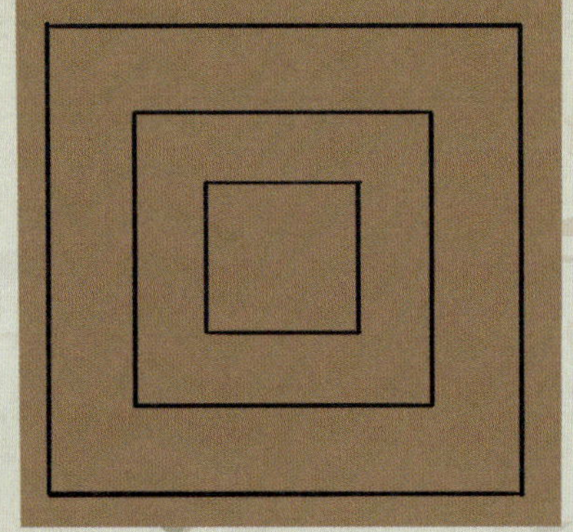

Draw three squares.

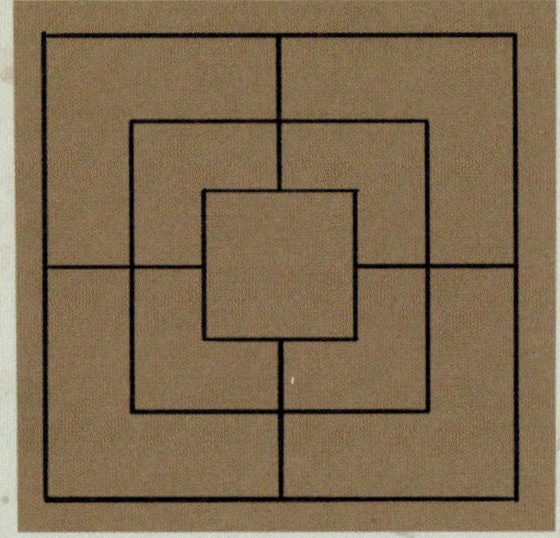

Connect the squares with lines.

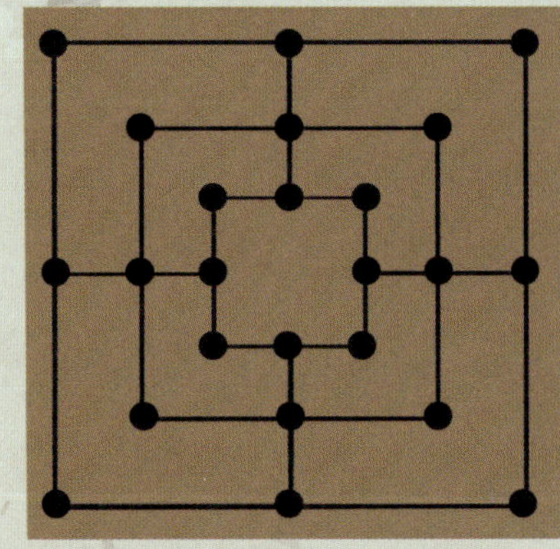

Draw dots at each of the 24 intersections.

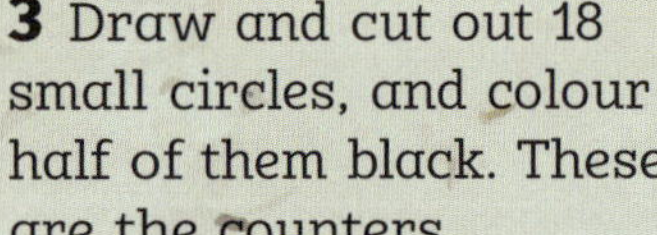

How to play:

- Players take turns placing their counters onto the intersections, trying to get a row of three. If they do, they can permanently remove one of the other player's pieces from the game.
- Once all the counters are on the board, players take turns sliding their counters along the lines, from one intersection to the next. Again, the aim is to try to make a row of three and remove one of the other player's counters.
- Once a player has only three counters left, they can move their counters from any intersection to another one.
- The game ends when one player only has two counters left. The other player is the winner!

Other Tudor games

Here are some other Tudor games you could play.

Shovepenny

Shovegroat (now known as shovepenny) involved players sliding a coin across a table and trying to get it to stop at a particular point. To play it yourself, place a coin on one edge of a table, then try to slide it across so that it ends up as close to the other edge as possible, without falling off.

Dice game

One popular Tudor dice game was called One and Thirty. Each player rolls two dice as many times as they like, adding up the numbers as they go. The aim is to get as close to 31 as possible, without going over. The player who gets closest to 31 wins.

Quoits

In the game of quoits, players attempt to throw hoops over a stake in the ground. You can make your own hoops by tying three sticks together with string. Poke another stick upright into the ground as your target.

A TUDOR PLAYHOUSE

A trip to the theatre was a popular day out in Elizabethan London. It was a place to see and be seen, to escape work and worries, to chat with friends and be entertained. All sorts of people, from wealthy nobles to servants, came to soak up the spectacle.

England's first theatres

The country's very first theatre was built in London in 1576, and others soon followed, including the famous Globe Theatre. Before these theatres existed, plays were performed by groups of actors in the courtyards of inns, in market halls, at court and in the halls of great houses.

The religious plays that were common at the start of the Tudor period were gradually replaced by history plays, comedies (stories with happy endings) and tragedies (stories with unhappy endings and a lot of blood!)

A master of words

William Shakespeare was one of the most famous playwrights of Elizabethan England. He wrote almost 40 plays, including *Romeo and Juliet* and *Macbeth*, and invented hundreds of new words, including 'moonbeams' and 'bedroom'. Shakespeare was one of the owners of a theatre company called The Lord Chamberlain's Men, which performed at the Globe Theatre. Sometimes he even acted on stage himself.

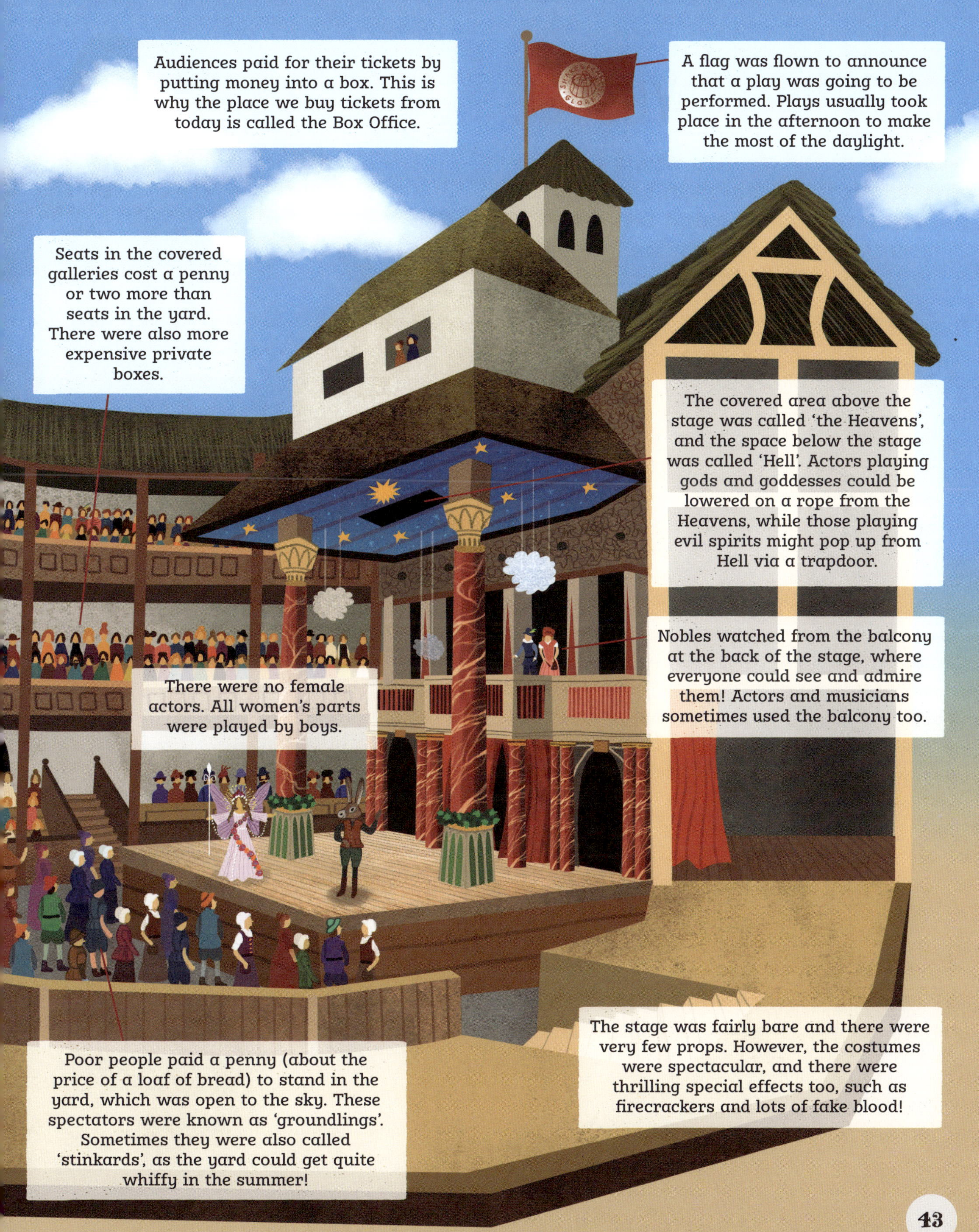

Audiences paid for their tickets by putting money into a box. This is why the place we buy tickets from today is called the Box Office.
A flag was flown to announce that a play was going to be performed. Plays usually took place in the afternoon to make the most of the daylight.
Seats in the covered galleries cost a penny or two more than seats in the yard. There were also more expensive private boxes.
The covered area above the stage was called 'the Heavens', and the space below the stage was called 'Hell'. Actors playing gods and goddesses could be lowered on a rope from the Heavens, while those playing evil spirits might pop up from Hell via a trapdoor.
Nobles watched from the balcony at the back of the stage, where everyone could see and admire them! Actors and musicians sometimes used the balcony too.
There were no female actors. All women's parts were played by boys.
The stage was fairly bare and there were very few props. However, the costumes were spectacular, and there were thrilling special effects too, such as firecrackers and lots of fake blood!
Poor people paid a penny (about the price of a loaf of bread) to stand in the yard, which was open to the sky. These spectators were known as 'groundlings'. Sometimes they were also called 'stinkards', as the yard could get quite whiffy in the summer!

A TRIP TO THE THEATRE

I am so excited I could burst! My father has brought us to the new playhouse that's opened on the far bank of the River Thames. There must be thousands of people here! Some are sitting up in the galleries, but most are crowded together in the yard below the stage, packed shoulder to shoulder in the hot sun. I feel grateful for my shady seat high above the stage. At first, it felt strange to have hundreds of pairs of curious eyes gazing at me, pointing at my dress and my jewellery, but I soon forget to be self-conscious – there is so much to see!

Down in the crowd I spot ale and pie sellers hollering for customers, a mother jiggling a wailing baby, friends laughing and clapping each other on the back, and people pushing and shoving to get a better spot. A group of young men holding tankards of ale are singing loudly and sloshing their ale onto the dirt floor. Over by one of the entrances a loud cry breaks out as a young boy pelts out of the

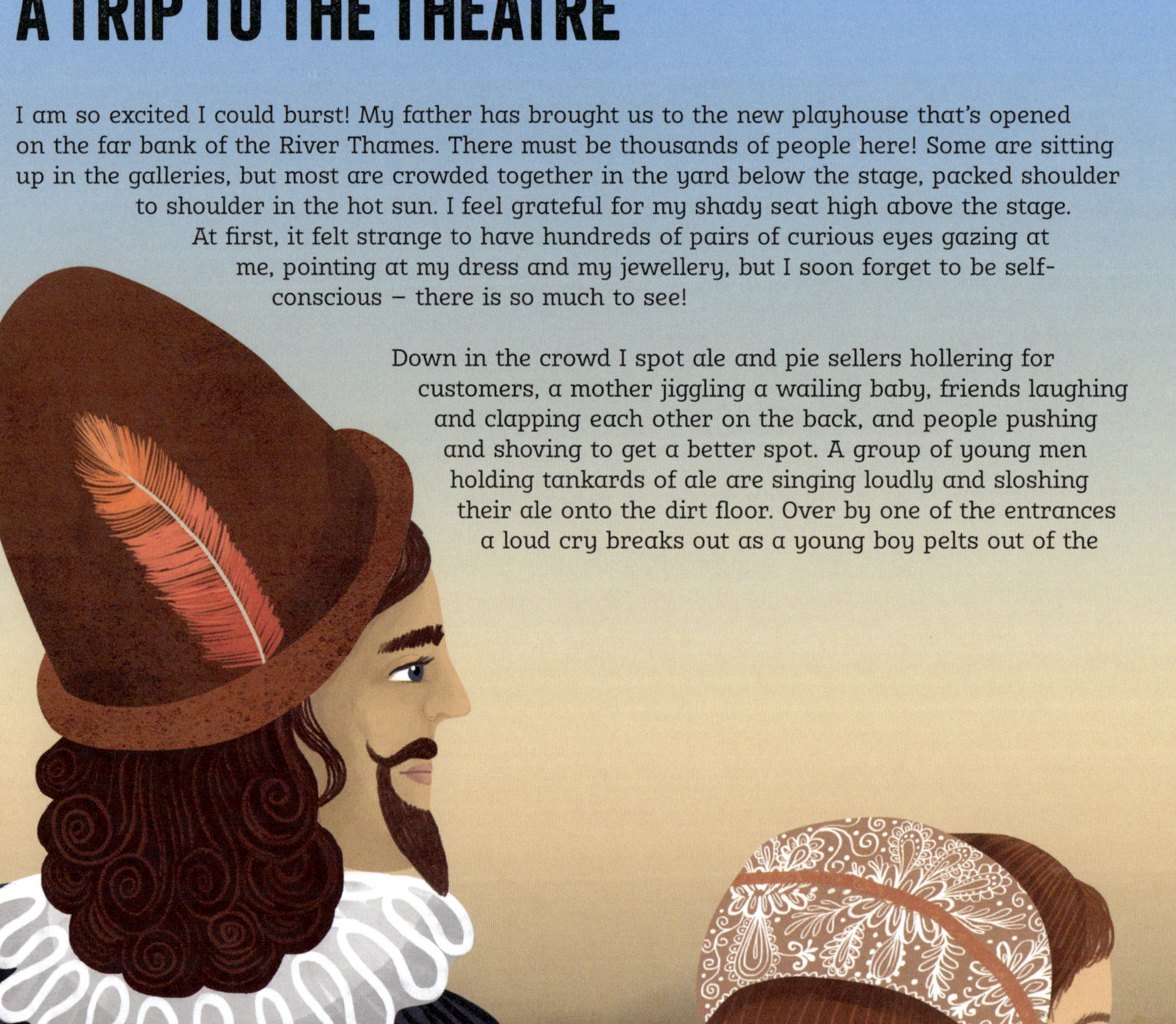

theatre, chased by an angry man yelling "Stop him! Thief!" A smell of garlic, beer and unwashed bodies wafts up from the crowd.

Suddenly, a trumpet sounds, and a hush falls over the playhouse – the play is about to begin! For the next few hours, the crowd cheers and laughs and gasps as the actors tell the story of the great Roman ruler, Julius Caesar. At one point, I almost jump out of my skin when a loud rumble shakes the stage, accompanied by a bright flash. Seconds later, someone in the audience screams as a firecracker shoots down a wire from the top of the stage to the bottom. My heart only stops thudding when I realize there is a thunderstorm in the play, and the noises and flashes are thunder and lightning!

Later, I have to cover my eyes and peek through my fingers in the scene when Caesar is killed by a group of nobles. The actor playing Caesar sinks to his knees, howling, as knives flash all around him and blood spurts in great crimson gushes over the stage. It all looks so real that I feel a bit sick, but the audience seems to love it – they boo the assassins enthusiastically. In another scene, one of the actors keeps forgetting his lines. Some of the groundlings begin to jeer him, and an apple core sails up out of the crowd and bounces off the poor actor's head.

When the play finally ends, everyone cheers loudly, and the actors take to the stage again to sing and dance. My father tells me one of the actors is also the playwright. He is called William Shakespeare. I wonder if he will write any more plays?

FOOD AND DRINK

In Tudor times, what people ate depended on their position in society. The simple meals of a farmer were very different from the lavish feasts of the nobility. Even amongst the well-off, there were rules about the number of dishes that could be served – the more important the person, the more they were allowed!

What people ate

Most people in Tudor times ate fairly simple food: bread, vegetables, pottage (a thick soup), butter and cheese, eggs, honey and small amounts of meat and fish. Weak beer was drunk by everyone, even children – it was sweet, thick and filling. In the winter, people had to rely on foods they had stored, such as pickled vegetables and dried or smoked meat.

Wealthy Tudors got to enjoy a much bigger range of foods, including luxuries imported from abroad, such as citrus fruits, almonds, spices and sugar. An enormous amount of meat was eaten too – lamb, pork, beef, venison, rabbit, badger, wild boar, goose, duck, heron, swan, thrush, and more. In fact, it's estimated that 80% of the nobility's diet was protein!

Fish Fridays!

In 1563, Elizabeth I passed a law that everyone had to eat fish instead of meat on Wednesdays, Fridays and Saturdays. This was to support the fishing industry, because England's navy needed experienced sailors.

Mealtimes and manners

Most people ate three meals: a light breakfast, dinner (the main meal, eaten around 11am or noon), and supper (a smaller meal at the end of the working day). In middle-class and well-off households, meals were usually two courses. Each course was made up of several different dishes, such as roasted and boiled meats, pottage, tarts and pies, custards and jellies. These dishes were served in portions for four people, called 'messes', which were set along the table for people to help themselves. People ate using their fingers, spoons and knives (forks weren't used until the 17th century).

Table manners were very important. Everyone knew to wash their hands before eating, wipe their fingers on a napkin, talk politely to their neighbour and sit still without wriggling. One manners book written for children even covered the tricky problem of needing to fart at the table – if it can't be helped, the author wrote, "let a cough hide the explosive sound".

New foods

During the Tudor Age, new foods found their way across the ocean from the Americas, including potatoes, kidney beans, pumpkins and turkey. Tomatoes (known as 'love apples') arrived too, but the Tudors didn't eat them as they thought they were poisonous!

TUDOR RECIPES

England's first printed recipe books were written in the Tudor Age. The recipes weren't very detailed though – usually, there were no measurements, no ingredient lists and no cooking times! Here are some Tudor recipes you can try out for yourself.

Tarte Owt of Lent

This tart gets its name from the fact it is made using ingredients that people weren't allowed to eat during Lent (the six weeks before Easter).

Ingredients

- **17½oz (500g) shortcrust pastry**
- **7oz (200g) Cheshire cheese**
- **10½oz (300g) double cream**
- **2 eggs, beaten**
- **salt and pepper**
- **beaten egg yolk (for glazing)**

1 Preheat the oven to 350°F (160°C fan). Grease a pie dish with butter.

2 Roll out two-thirds of the pastry and place it in the dish, covering the base and sides.

3 Use your fingers to crumble up the cheese as finely as you can into a big bowl.

4 Add the eggs, cream, salt and pepper and mix everything together. Pour into the pastry case.

5 Roll out the rest of pastry to make a lid for the pie. Brush the edges of the pie base with egg yolk, then place the pie lid on top and pinch the edges together. Trim any spare pastry, and brush the pie lid with egg yolk.

6 Bake at 350°F (160°C fan) for 30–40 minutes or until the pie is golden brown.

Mad, bad Tudor recipes

Not all Tudor recipes were as tasty as the ones on these pages! Cooks liked to combine sweet and savoury flavours, sometimes with strange results. Would you fancy eating a pickled fish and fig tart, or calf's-foot jelly flavoured with spices and rosewater? Other bizarre dishes include 'surprise pie' – a pastry case filled with live frogs or blackbirds. When the pie lid was removed, the animals would hop or fly away, giving the guests quite a shock!

Shrewsbury biscuits

These tasty biscuits are flavoured with rosewater, which was a popular ingredient in Tudor times.

Ingredients

Makes 8 biscuits

- **8oz (225g) plain flour**
- **3½oz (100g) caster sugar**
- **½ tsp cinnamon**
- **4½oz (125g) butter, cut into small cubes**
- **1 egg, beaten**
- **½ tsp rosewater**

1 Preheat the oven to 320°F (140°C fan).

2 Mix together all of the dry ingredients in a big bowl, then use your fingers to rub in the butter.

3 Use a spoon to mix in the beaten egg and rosewater.

4 Knead the mixture on a floured worksurface until it forms a stiff dough.

5 Divide the dough into 8 balls, and pat them into thin rounds about 5in (12cm) wide.

6 Place the biscuits on two greased baking trays and bake for around 15 minutes.

Spiced pears

The Tudors didn't think it was healthy to eat pears raw, but they enjoyed them cooked with wine, sugar and spices. In this recipe, we've used red grape juice instead of wine.

Ingredients

- **4 pears**
- **18fl oz (500ml) red grape juice**
- **3½fl oz (100ml) honey**
- **2 tsp ground cinnamon**
- **2 tsp ground ginger**

1 Mix the juice, honey and spices in a saucepan, and heat.

2 Peel the pears, then add them to the pan.

3 Simmer gently with the lid on, turning the pears from time to time until they are cooked (around 30 minutes).

A TUDOR CHRISTMAS

Tudor Christmases were celebrated for twelve days, from December 25 through to January 5th, which was known as Twelfth Night. Christmas was a time when everyone took a break from work, visited friends and had fun! This is how our Tudor friend Mary might have celebrated Christmas.

24th December (Christmas Eve)

The house looks beautiful this evening. Everywhere I look there are garlands of holly, ivy and mistletoe. Tomorrow we will light the huge Yule log that lies in the great hearth – it must have taken the servants hours to drag it back from the woods this morning. I can't wait for tomorrow. For forty days we've had no meat, no eggs, no cheese. But tomorrow I'm going to eat until I burst out of my laces!

25th December (Christmas Day)

We rose early to go to church this morning, and when we returned home the Yule log was blazing and the house was filled with the smell of spices and roasted meats.

Once we took our places in the hall, the musicians began to play and the steward carried in the great boar's head and set it down in front of my father. Then the feast began! There was plum porridge, roasted venison, mince pies, a peacock clothed in its feathers, platters piled high with wobbling jellies, gingerbread and marzipan. And my favourite, Christmas pie – a turkey stuffed with a goose stuffed with a chicken stuffed with a partridge stuffed with a pigeon!

After we ate, there was dancing and singing, and the servants brought in the wassail bowl, filled to the brim with steaming spiced punch. Cheers and song rang out as it passed from person to person, each drinker calling out 'Wassail!' – 'your good health!'

Tomorrow, we will give the leftover food to the poor.

1st January (New Year's Day)

Today is gift-giving day. My father is at court, where all the noble families will be presenting their gift to the Queen. I got a gift from my parents too: a pair of beautiful embroidered slippers.

5th January (Twelfth Night)

Guess what happened today? When the Twelfth Night cake was carried in at the end of the feast, we all cut a slice, hoping to find the hidden bean baked inside. And do you know who found it and became Queen of the Bean? Me!! My father let me sit at the head of the table and lead the singing.

Afterwards, we watched acrobats tumble across the hall and fire-eaters breathe great bursts of flames. My mother couldn't stop glancing at the tapestries – I think she was worried about them catching fire. I wanted to stay up and watch the play afterwards, but I was so tired I could hardly keep my eyes open.

Tomorrow we will take down the decorations, and Christmas will be over for another year.

COULD YOU HAVE LIVED LIKE A TUDOR?

Life could be tough in Tudor times, especially if you were poor or ill, or got into trouble with the law! Do you think you would have liked to live like a Tudor? Think about the questions here and talk about your answers with a friend, parent, carer or teacher.

1 Many Tudor children left home as teenagers to live in other households. It was a chance to meet new people, see new places, learn new skills and earn money, but it might have felt scary too. How do think you would have felt leaving the family home? What sort of household would you have liked to move to, and what work would *you* have liked to do?

2 More and more people lived in towns in the Tudor Age, but most of the population still lived in the countryside. Where would you have preferred to live: a big city (smelly and crowded, but with lots of shops and entertainment) or a tiny village (peaceful; every day is much the same and everyone knows everyone)?

3 If you time-travelled back to Tudor times, what three things do you think you would miss the most from your modern-day life? It might be certain gadgets or foods, things you like to do, or comforts like a hot shower or a flushing toilet! Is there anything you'd like to take from the time of the Tudors and bring back to the modern world?

4 Tudor punishments for law-breakers were very harsh. Do you think they were always fair? Take a look at the Tudor punishments below. How would these crimes be treated today? Are they all crimes? How would you judge each crime?

- Not going to church regularly – a fine
- Stealing an apple – whipping
- Stealing a purse of money – execution (hanging)
- Gossiping about a neighbour – cucking stool
- Following the wrong religion – execution (burned at stake)
- Begging for food – whipping or execution

5 Imagine you are hosting a Tudor dinner party. Plan all the fancy dishes you will serve your guests: you will need two courses, each with five dishes. You can choose your own dishes if you like, or come up with some weird and wonderful creations of your own.

6 Just like today, there were a variety of jobs in Tudor England. Which of the following would you rather be?

- An explorer setting sail to discover new lands – you might come back rich and famous... or you might not come back at all!
- A craftsperson living comfortably above their shop in London
- A noblewoman – you live in luxury, but everything you own belongs to your husband, and you didn't get to choose who you married
- An actor working at one of London's new theatres
- The groom of the stool – this courtier's job is highly sought after. Helping the king go to the toilet means you spend a lot of time with him, which makes you very important and influential!

7 At school, young children were taught how to read and write using the alphabet and Bible verses (story books didn't exist yet). Lessons were generally learnt by repeating them over and over again, and teachers were very strict. How do Tudor lessons compare to lessons in your school?

8 In the 16th century, Christmas celebrations lasted for twelve days. Plan your own twelve days of Tudor fun and entertainment! Who would you see and what would you do on each day?

GLOSSARY

apothecary
A person who in the past made and sold medicines.

apprentice
A person who works with someone so that they can learn how to do the job themselves.

bled (medical treatment)
When a doctor 'bled' a patient, they cut open a vein and let the blood drip into a bowl or put bloodsucking leeches onto the skin. Bloodletting was used as a medical treatment for over 2,000 years, until the late 19th century.

Catholic
Relating to the Catholic Church. Catholicism is the largest branch of Christianity and is led by the Pope.

cesspit
A hole in the ground used for human waste.

chamber pot
A bowl kept in the bedroom and used as a toilet at night.

Church of England
The official Church in England, created by Henry VIII in 1534. The head of the Church is the English king or queen.

civil war
A war fought between people of the same country.

colonies
Countries or areas that are under the control of another more powerful country, which sends its own people to settle there.

convent
A place where a religious community of nuns live and work.

courtier
A person who is a member of a king or queen's court.

enslaved people
Woman, men or children who are owned as property by someone else and made to work for them without pay.

estate
An area of land in the countryside, usually with a large house, which is owned by a wealthy person or family.

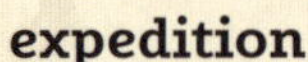

expedition
A long journey made for a particular reason, for example, to explore or to make scientific discoveries.

fasting
To go willingly without food or certain foods for an amount of time, often for religious reasons.

heresy
Having religious beliefs that are different from the official religion.

Latin
A language that was spoken in the Roman Empire around 2,000 years ago. In the Tudor Age, Latin was used in official documents, Catholic church services and more.

lute
A musical instrument with strings, which is played a bit like a guitar. It was a very popular instrument in Europe in the 16th and 17th centuries.

maid of honour
A young, unmarried woman whose job it was to serve the queen. Usually, maids of honour came from noble families.

merchant
A person who travels from place to place, buying and selling goods.

monastery
A place where a religious community of monks live and work.

nobility (also nobles, noblemen)
The second-most important rank of Tudor society, just beneath the king or queen. Noblemen had titles (such as Baron, Duke or Earl), were very wealthy and generally owned big country estates.

parliament
The group of people who make the laws for a country.

playwright
A person who writes plays.

ploughs
Large tools used by farmers to loosen and turn over the soil before seeds are planted.

Presence Chamber
The room in a Tudor palace where the king or queen received guests. It was connected to the monarch's private apartments (Privy Chamber).

Protestant
Relating to Protestantism, which is the second-largest branch of Christianity. The first Protestant churches developed in the 16th century, when some people began to break away from the Catholic Church.

rushes
Grasslike plants which grow in bogs and marshes.

spindle
A tool used to twist wool and turn it into thread.

stocks (trading)
Stocks are tiny pieces of ownership in a company. When you buy a stock, you are buying a small piece of that company.

superstition
A belief that isn't based on fact and can't be explained by reason or science.

tapestries
Thick, heavy pieces of woven or embroidered cloth. In Tudor times, wealthy people decorated their homes with huge tapestries hung on the walls. Designs often showed repeating patterns, animals, plants, fruits or scenes from stories.

tiltyard
A field used for jousting contests. The barrier that separates the competitors is called a 'tilt'.

treason
The crime of betraying your country (king, queen or government) by doing something that harms it or puts it in danger, such as helping its enemies.

ABOUT THE AUTHOR

Claire Saunders has been writing and editing books for more than 20 years. Specializing in children's non-fiction, she has authored or co-authored many titles including *Live Like a Roman, Live Like a Viking and Live Like an Ancient Egyptian* (for Button Books), *The Power Book, The Birthday Almanac, A World of Gratitude* and various activity books, including the *Africana Activity Book*, the *National Monuments of the USA Activity Book* and the *Football Fantastic Activity Book.* A graduate of Cambridge University, she has previously worked for Ivy Press and Rough Guides and still loves travelling the world, learning about the history of other cultures. She lives with her family in Lewes, southern England.

Acknowledgements

Thanks to Dr Emilie Murphy for her expert knowledge and help.

First published 2025 by Button Books, an imprint of Guild of Master Craftsman Publications Ltd, Castle Place, 166 High Street, Lewes, East Sussex, BN7 1XU, UK. Text © Claire Saunders, 2025. Copyright in the Work © GMC Publications Ltd, 2025. ISBN 978 1 78708 177 2. Distributed by Publishers Group West in the United States. A catalogue record for this book is available from the British Library. Publisher: Jonathan Bailey, Production: Jim Bulley, Senior Project Editor: Susie Behar, Design Manager: Robin Shields, Designer: Emily Hurlock, Illustrator: Mia Underwood. Colour origination by GMC Reprographics. Printed and bound in China.

BUTTON BOOKS

For more on Button Books, contact:
GMC Publications Ltd, Castle Place,
166 High Street, Lewes, East Sussex,
BN7 1XU, United Kingdom
Tel: +44 (0)1273 488005
buttonbooks.co.uk/buttonbooks.us